A CHILDREN'S STORY METAPHORICALLY WRITTEN TO SHOW HOW POWERFUL PRAYER IS FOR A CHILD

Scripture from which I came is Colossians 4:1 "Devote yourselves to prayer, being watchful and thankful". NIV

A NOTE TO THE PARENTS.

CHILDREN ARE YOUNG AND IMPRESSIONABLE. CHILDREN CAN'T GRASPS THE POWER OF THEIR PRAYER IN STRENGTH. SO GOD GAVE ME A WAY TO DRAW OUT FOR CHILDREN A MENTAL PICTURE.

I HOPE AND PRAY THIS WILL ENCOURAGE THEM TO PRAY MORE WITH AN UNDERSTANDING OF HOW POWERFUL THEIR PRAYERS ARE; AND YOU AS THE PARENT...I PRAY THAT YOU TOO WILL FEEL THE STRENGTH THAT CAN BE DRAWN FROM THIS WONDERFUL WAY TO VIEW THE POWER OF PRAYER, FOR PRAYER IS AN ACTION, IN POWER AND IN SPIRIT.

AMEN!

MY DESIRE IS TO GIVE GOD THE GLORY IN ALL I DO FOR CHILDREN OF ALL AGES, YOUNG AND OLD. I BELIEVE THIS BOOK IS AN ADDED BLESSING TO THE KINGDOM.

PRAYER IS STRONG AND BIG AS AN ELEPHANT

Text copyright © 2004 by Lorraine Munerlyn

Illustrations copyright © 2004 by Lorraine Munerlyn

All rights reserved. No part of this book may be used or reproduced in any manner without written permission from the author.

For information about permission to reproduce selections from the book, write to Poet/Artist Lorraine Munerlyn, P.O. Box 4203, Flint, MI 48504-3367

Published by G Publishing, LLC
Detroit, Michigan

Printed in the United States

ISBN: 0-9717519-1-9

Library of Congress Control Number: 2006922924

ACKNOWLEDGMENTS

I GIVE GOD ALL THE HONOR, GLORY AND PRAISE FOR MY FIRST CHILDREN'S BOOK, AND I THANK THE CHILDREN OF PROMISE AT NBM FOR HELPING ME UNDERSTAND HOW IMPORTANT IT IS FOR CHILDREN TO UNDERSTAND THERE IS POWER IN THEIR PRAYERS, AND HOW STRONG THEIR PRAYER'S ARE.

I GIVE THANKS ALSO TO MY DEAR SISTER IN CHRIST, BETTY WINGFIELD.

INTRODUCING TO CHILDREN THE POWER OF A CHILD'S PRAYER

PRAYER IS STRONG AND BIG AS AN ELEPHANT

In the animal kingdom, there are many animals that are created by God. In fact, God says in His Word "Let everything that has breath praise His Holy Name". Psalm 150

God caused me to think about children; and how many children think about prayer? Not many, except for those that are being taught to pray. Do they really understand how powerful prayer is, especially the children that are at the age of 6-12yrs. old?

From the animal kingdom, God and I selected the elephant, to depict to a child how strong their power in prayer is.

All Children know from picture books, and from watching animal planet, that elephants are strong, and powerful, and they're able to move big things, but very gentle, kind, and loving.

The prayer of a child is big and strong, just like an elephant. Prayers strong enough to reach God in heaven.

God says in His Holy Word, "In all thy getting get an understanding". God desires for children to understand how BIG and POWERFUL their PRAYERS really are, and it's never too early to start teaching them to pray.

Thank you for taking the time to read to a child.

When you pray, in your mind you're picturing different things that God might be like.

So when you pray, you're imagining Him to be all sorts of things, like tall trees, fluffy clouds in the sky, but none of these things has breath to praise God in songs to sing.

God is your prayers that are big as an elephant.

Hearing all your prayers with His big beautiful ears, listening to the prayers of a world of children everyday of every year.

1900 December
1809 November
2008
September 2000
2004 October
1929 August
1999 July
B.C.
2010
2001 June
A.C.
1961 Febuary
1988
1957 April
1958 January
March 2006
May 1984

God is the flowers. He's the grass that feels soft under your bare feet, as you run and laugh with songs to sing.

There's a little bit of God in everything!

So if God is all these people, places and things, then you can picture God in your prayer being strong and big as an elephant.

They don't know that their prayer is big and strong as an elephant, prayers strong enough to reach all the way to heaven.

All you have to do is pray to God anytime and anywhere, and God will hear your prayers, because your prayer is strong and big as an elephant reaching God's ears in heaven.

God can hear the prayers of a child from anywhere.

Repenting is saying, "I'm sorry," to God and to people when we're wrong or when we've hurt them. That's the right thing to do, when you know you've been bad, mean, and just plain old cruel.

You can measure your power of prayer by thinking of prayer being as big and strong as an elephant; but yet kind and gentle in strength, lifting up all things in prayer to reach heaven.

Elephants have good memory; they live long as people, and they have this quiet sound that they make to communicate with each other up to 6 miles away from each other, a sound that only can be heard by them and God, not by children.

God is much farther away, but He loves children so much, and because He created prayer, He can hear thousands of miles away, answering everyone who prays with a heart that's sincere.

Children have the same way of communicating with God too. Children that pray from their hearts are giving God all their troubles, and worries, and only God and Jesus can hear a child's prayer, because people are not strong like God, and people fail to imagine their prayers being strong and big as an elephant.

A CHILD'S PRAYER TO GOD

Father God, I am your child.

I desire to do your will on earth, as it is in heaven,

Giving You all the honor and Glory.

Help me everyday, Father God, to draw nigh to You, so that You will draw nigh to me.

Help me to always turn my back on sin, and turn to You with a heart of repentance.

In Jesus Name amen.

THE END.

PRAYER IS STRONG AND BIG AS AN ELEPHANT
DEFINITION PAGE

THERE ARE SOME WORDS THAT ARE IN THIS BOOK; YOU AS A CHILD
MAY NOT UNDERSTAND WHAT THE WORDS MEAN,
SO HERE ARE SOME WORDS DEFINED FOR YOU. THEY ARE ALSO IN THE BIBLE.

1. THE WORD PETITION MEANS - TO SIGN UP, MAKING A REQUEST KNOWN IN WRITING. (1 JOHN 5:15)

2. THE WORD REPENTANCE MEANS - REMORSE, or SORRY. (EXODUS 10:17)

3. THE WORD DRAW IN THE BIBLE MEANS - TO PULL, or ATTRACT LIKE A MAGNET; MEANING IT IS IN GOD'S LOVING-KINDNESS THAT GOD PULLS YOU CLOSER TO HIM. (JEREMIAH 31:3)

4. THE WORD NIGH MEANS - CLOSE TO, or NEAR; GOD IS ALREADY THINKING ABOUT YOU, HE WANTS YOU TO CLEANSE YOUR HANDS FROM SINS AND GIVE HIM YOUR HEART AND MIND. (JAMES 4:8)

5. THE WORD OPPRESSION MEANS - A FEELING OF BEING WEIGHED DOWN, BY SOMETHING OR SOMEONE. (PSALM 119:134)

6. THE WORD DEPRESSION MEANS - A FEELING OF BEING DEPRESSED IN YOUR FEELINGS, YOU DON'T FEEL LIKE LAUGHING OR SINGING. (NEHEMIAH 2:2)

7. THE WORD CONFUSION MEANS - DISORDER OR JUST SIMPLY NOT UNDERSTANDING. (JAMES 3:16)

8. THE WORD DIVORCE MEANS - TO DISSOLVE THE MARRIAGE BOND BETWEEN TWO PEOPLE. (DEUTERONOMY 24:1)

9. THE WORD POWER MEANS - TO BE STRONG NATURALLY, AND IN SPIRIT. WHEN WE PRAY FROM THE HEART WE ARE PRAYING WITH GOD'S POWER. (JOHN 19:11)

Printed in the United States
143609LV00005B